CW00369797

INTRODUCTION

For this my eighteenth book in the Around series I have returned to the Bath and North-Ea
in particular to the three small communities of High Littleton, Hallatrow and Farrington Gu.....
to interlock new books with those previously published, and in this case the story starts in Farmborough and also links in
with Temple Cloud *(see Around Timsbury)* as I invite you to take a pictorial journey around this beautiful part of our local
environs. Although Hallatrow is regarded as a hamlet and accordingly much smaller than its neighbour High Littleton, it
is much older than the adjacent community, having been identified in the Domesday Book as Helgetreu which is believed
to be Saxon for Holy tree. Whether there is any connection with Joseph of Arimathea, his staff and the Glastonbury thorn
is not known even though it has been suggested that cuttings may have been taken from the Glastonbury thorn and planted
in other parts of Somerset, including Hallatrow, but again there is no evidence to support this hypothesis. High Littleton
and Farrington Gurney were also mentioned in the Domesday Book, implying that all three localities covered by this
book were founded on agriculture. Subsequently the discovery of coal further developed the growth of the villages although
known to the Romans where it was found on the surface, its importance was not fully appreciated for many hundreds of
years, and it was not until the latter part of the eighteenth century that technical engineering improvements enabled coal
to be dug at greater depths, and perhaps more importantly that it could be conveyed to the market place in large quantities
at relatively cheap prices; and. within a hundred years or so, there were at least twenty mines within walking distance of
the three communities covered by this book. High Littleton was probably conceived by the Saxons around the beginning
of the eight-century on a 500ft. hill that dominated the surrounding area making it a valuable place for defence and tracking
the movement of others. The church of Holy Trinity was originally built during the first half of the twelve century and then
partially rebuilt in 1888 some fifty-five years after the construction of the nearby elementary school to accommodate 75
children. Farrington is also listed in the Domesday, and probably did not adopt the second part of its name until the eleventh
century, when St John the Baptist was constructed under the auspices of the Gourney family. Subsequently the church was
rebuilt and enlarged in 1843, with its school being constructed in 1852, and enlarged to accommodate 119 pupils in 1894.

The preparation of this book would not have been possible without the help of those kind ladies who pointed me in the
right direction to identify the position of the old photographs; Sheila Brooks for reading and correcting the transcript and
Ken Scotcher for allowing me to use some of his pictures, and for his brother Roy for making suitable copies. At all times
I have endeavoured to minimise any mistakes made but should any exist then they are unfortunately of my own making,
for which I apologise and trust that they will not distract you from enjoying the remaining contents.

September 2011   Ian S. Bishop

Three young children including one on a tricycle, with a slightly older boy watch with interest as the photographer sets up his equipment that will capture this moment in time forever. On the right is the frontage of the seventeenth century Manor House, whilst beyond an elderly gentleman appears around *Brook Vale,* c1908

As we are invited to look along The Street towards the centre of Farmborough, a pony and trap with two ladies on board is about to start the climb of this steep section of Bath Road as the *Olds Bell* stands out proudly on the skyline, whilst a steam lorry is about to descend the hill, c1910.

New Road, High Littleton.

The entrance to High Littleton from Bath as we look down New Road built in the 1820's as a more direct turnpike road into the village. On the right are the petrol pumps and advertising board belonging to the garage premises of motor engineer Sidney Young, whilst beyond is the house known as *Upper Sixpence* with the taller buildings being 1-4 Fair View, c1933

New Road, High Littleton.

The camera has been moved further into the village and turned completely around as we are invited to glance back along New Road, and to study at our leisure a view that starts with the property now known as *Santoy* on the left and *Indalo* and *The Linney* on the right. No traffic, no road markings, no street furniture provides us with a peaceful scene that will never be replicated today, c1932.

HIGH LITTLETON
X12

Again the camera has been moved back, but the young woman who has been asked to stand in the middle of the road has, despite the complete absence of any traffic, become nervous and not stood as still as the photographer would wish. In this view we can see more of the properties as we approach the junction with Scrumrum Lane, c1908

We have now reached the junction of New Road with Scrumrum Lane, which up to the second decade of the nineteenth century was known as Combesham Lane and was the main route out of High Littleton on the turnpike to Bath. With just one parked car, there was, when this picture was taken around 1933, no need for traffic management signs to untidy this pleasant view.

New Road, High Littleton.

6

Looking along the High Street from the junction with Greyfield Road we have on the left the *High Littleton Inn,* with two horseless carts loaded with quarried stone. It is possible that both horses have been unhitched and taken to the stable for food and water, whilst the carters have probably not given up the opportunity of finding their own refreshments in the hostelry, c1910.

Although there appears little activity in this view of Greyfield Colliery, there is plenty of activity going on underground, despite the fact that the colliery will close in about nine years time. Note the double wooden headgear, the winding engine house, and a puff of smoke coming away from the Cornish engine house, c1902

An active scene at Greyfield Colliery showing at the head of a variety of private owner's wagons its 0-4.0 locomotive *Daisy*, as it manoeuvres them around in front of the shaft and winding engine. Opened in the 1830's the colliery was the scene of major flooding in 1909, which broke through from adjoining old workings causing the death of six pit ponies, but no miners. *Daisy* arrived in 1894 and stayed on site until the mine closed in 1911.The picture probably dates from around 1902.

High Street, High Littleton. No.2.

8267

We have now passed the Methodist Church on the left, turned the camera completely around and pulled up outside Tom Harris's newsagents shop with beyond *The Chimes* and *Pioneer Cottage;* opposite is a cottage that offered bed and breakfast and was where the author of the card was staying, c1935

Steve and Eileen Harris proudly stand in the doorway of Tom Harris's newsagent/tobacconist's shop, which according to the right-hand window display also acts as a haberdashery business, c1934. Today the building is occupied by Emz Hair Studio.

High Street, High Littleton.

The camera has been moved further along the High Street to give us this more panoramic view. On the left is Tom Harris's shop; whilst on the right is the post office and butchers run by Frank Blinman, c1928

High Street, High Littleton.

Another panoramic view of the High Street as we continue to look in the general direction of Bath. It is believed that the shop on the right belonged to Mrs Emma Curtis. Note the precariously perched lady cleaning her upstairs' windows on the left; what would health and safety make of it today!, c1930

High Street, High Littleton.

There is just one open-top car in this otherwise view of a deserted High Street; how peaceful the village once was. On the right a sign advertising Cleveland petrol at 1/2d (less than 0.06p) per gallon, but it is unlikely that there will be many takers, as it will take forty years or more before the High Street is swamped by the infernal combustion engine, c1935

14

Although the camera has been hardly moved, we are taken back in time in this picture when compared with the previous views. Yet to arrive are the poles and wires bringing electricity /telephones to the village, but in this shot we are given the opportunity of seeing a gent sitting astride his bicycle as he balances with the aid of the gateposts, whilst looking on are two gentlemen both major amputees, in wheelchairs, possibly ex-wounded soldiers from the First World War, c1922

Having had the opportunity of studying the High Street in the general direction of Bath, the camera has now been turned completely around as we look towards *The Star* on the left with the cottages *Belmont* and *Glencoe* and the Wesleyan Chapel on the right; coming towards us are a couple on a motor scooter who have the whole of the road to themselves, c1950

A little closer to the Wesleyan Chapel, now the offices of Ken Biggs Contractors Ltd, are two Edwardian ladies happy to have their photograph taken as they stand in the middle of the road with a baby in a pram, not something that would be recommended today. Two girls fidget on the side, whilst a window cleaner keeps a watchful eye on the photographer, c1906

High St, High Littleton.

10988.

Much of this scene has now been taken from us with all of the buildings on the left as far as the first chapel having been demolished and the space now used as an area of car parking for Ken Biggs Contractors Ltd, who also use the taller building as their Headquarters. *The Star* public house is on the right, c1935

The cameraman has caused curious interest amongst a small group of village children, as the imposing eighteenth century *Pembroke House* dominates this view that includes in the distance The Batch. The date stone on the front of *Pembroke House* records the year 1777 (the sixteenth year of the reign of George 111) and although for most of its existence it has been a private house, there have been times when business such as hairdressing have taken place, including in the 1930's the dentist Henry Sampson performed his duties for an hour each Monday, c1910

The Batch, High Littleton.

The High Street and Timsbury Road is an area known locally as the Batch, and on the corner is a general shop run by Mrs Mary Couch that could, with the absence of significant motorised traffic be safely reached by both children and adults. To the right of the shop, but hidden from view is the *Old Market Tavern*, c1930

Architecturally shaped trees dominate this view of The Batch with the *Old Market Tavern* on the right behind the Somerset finger post. On the left it looks as though someone is being taught how to ride a bike, c1911

HIGH LITTLETON

In this aspect we have the chance to observe the bend of the road as it sweeps around to the High Street, whilst at the same time we are able to look down Timsbury Road. To help animate the picture the photographer has encouraged a number of villagers, including one with pony and trap to stand and stare, probably without realising that their image was about to be frozen in time, c1914

The Batch, High Littleton.

826

A grandfather and granddaughter hold hands as they stop quite safely in the road, and watch with interest as the photographer bends over the wooden tripod, covers his head with a black cloth and looks at a black and white upside down picture of The Batch and the large garden on the left although of course it will appear to his right, c1920

The Batch around 1909, showing a group of village children all neatly turned out, although two girls appear to be having a wrestling match at the junction with Timsbury Road. Stones seem to have been piled up in front of the wall surrounding the large tree on the right, giving a number of the children a higher platform on which to be seen, interestingly within the rank of cottages lived William Sage a stonemason. Taken from a postcard used as a Christmas 1910 card.

Students from years five and six of the High Littleton Church of England School pose for their group photograph together with two teachers outside of the main entrance with clock above the door, c1934

The church of Holy Trinity, built during the early fourteenth century in local stone in the Early Perpendicular 'style, complete with a chancel, a four bay nave, and an embattled western tower with pinnacles containing six bells. Possibly because of subsidence, both the chancel and the nave were rebuilt in 1739, and eighty-five years later a south aisle added, followed by a north aisle eighteen years latter. During the 1880'sour Victorian ancestors restored

and virtually rebuilt in their own way most of the church, How much more rural it once was with a narrow country road built for horse power counted in one's and two's as we reach the outskirts of the village, c1910. On the right is a view of the north side of Holy Trinity church as we look down the hill away from the centre of the village. The road has been widened, and the photographer has attracted a small group of young men from the village, c1921

A view of the well manicured lawn that sets off the attractive gardens surrounding Holy Trinity vicarage home of the Rev. A M Foster c1909

Well-matured elm trees in full summer foliage dominate this view of the A39 as the road passes on the right Mr Arthur Cox's *Rosewell Farm* and leaves the village of High Littleton as it is about to drop down to the hamlet of Hallatrow, c1910

A Bristol built 4-ton 28 seater single deck bus with solid tyres, coming down the hill from High Littleton on Route 88 Bristol to Radstock via Keynsham, is about to be overtaken by a car driver who no doubt believes the road belongs to him, and is unconcerned about meeting any oncoming traffic on its way up the hill, let alone the possibility of hitting the photographer who will, if the car keeps going, need to jump out of the way c1925

A general view of Hallatrow as we look up the hill towards High Littleton, taken from a card sent to Elm Tree Farm on the 6th September 1923.

Originally known as *Hallatrow Cottage* and lived in for a number of years by the Scobell family during the early nineteenth century, the property is now known as *The Grange.* Previously members of the Brodribb family had leased it. Probably built in the eighteenth century with the picture dating from around 1912.

Paulton Road sweeps around from its junction with the A39 Wells Road past *The Grange* with a splendid Dion Roadster, registration Y1603 parked outside, c1923

Woodview Cottages partially opened as an informal letter collecting office by William Brooks in the 1840's who also ran his carpentry business from the small building on the extreme right. The letters were brought from Bristol to Hallatrow by the local carrier and distributed around the nearby community by William, and within ten years he was elevated to the position of sub-postmaster with one of the front rooms becoming the village Post Office, where it remained in the Brooks family for the next seventy-five years, c1908

On the right we can see the ivy covered *Woodview Cottages* from a different angle including the smaller, almost lean-to type building on the left the home of one of William Brooks' daughters Henrietta and her husband until his death in 1943, although by then the Brooks family had handed over the role of sub-postmaster to Reginald Helliker who traded from new premises. Above on the left we are provided with a close-up of the attractive rural entrance to the original Post Office. The identity sign is almost covered by the ivy, the steps and pathway are fringed with flowers, and the main sign tells us that money orders; savings bank, and parcel post facilities exist, as well as insurance and annuity business, c1911

CROSS ROADS, HALLATROW.

Hallatrow crossroads at the meeting of Wells Road, looking in the direction of High Littleton, Hart's Lane and Paulton Road. Hiding behind the tress on the left is *Elm Cottage* whilst the foliage on the right hides *Woodview Cottages*, c1924

HALLATROW. CROSS ROADS.

The same crossroads showing a slightly different angle with the horse and carriage specifically placed in the sunshine to create a more atmospheric picture. The thatched building on the left has now been replaced by the property known as *Manor House,* and *Elm Cottage* is no longer hidden behind conifers, c1907

Hallatrow Court on the right, with *Yew Tree Cottage* on the left, as we look along Hart's Lane. On the facing side of the Court is a date stone of 1674 and the initials JD. However, from around 1725 the Brodribb family owned the property, and it remained in their hands for over two hundred years, c1925

MANOR FARM, HALLATROW.

Collinson, Clutton.

Previously known as *Hallatrow Farm* part of the building almost certainly dates back to the early 1500's when it was in the hands of the Rodney family. Over the centuries the building was extended and altered, but remained the main structural element of the Manor of Hallatrow, until the property, as seen on the left, was sold to the local transport entrepreneur Albert Stock in 1912, which is likely to coincide with the date of this picture.

Surely the person who owns the convertible touring car has not been caught speeding or excess drinking by the village policeman, as they gather together for this formal photograph to be taken outside the *Station Hotel*, perhaps he was just asking for directions, c1927

In this picture we are given a rare opportunity of seeing *Station Cottages,* an old part of Hallatrow that is sadly no longer with us. Probably built around 1820 we see them here around 1932, some twenty years or so before they were totally demolished to widen the road opposite the *Station Hotel.*

Parked in the grounds adjacent to the *Station Hotel* was this old four-wheeled railway carriage converted for use as their Mission Hall by the many Plymouth Brethren that lived in the area, c1912

In the early period of the station's existence the main line was single tracked for much of its length even as it went though Hallatrow station, which was a significant junction with the branch line to Camerton and substantial goods yard visible in the background behind the signal post, c1907

Hallatrow station and environs under went a major redevelopment programme during 1910/11, with the doubling of the track, the erection of a water tower, and the construction of a down platform, c1911

This charming picture taken from the down platform shows a mother and her three daughters all dressed in their Sunday best with many others from the nearby villages having a day away, and waiting for a train to take them perhaps to Weston-s-Mare, c1912

Looking down from the A39 road bridge the photographer has captured an ex-Great Western 0-6-0-pannier tank engine number 4607 and its two coaches leaving Hallatrow with a Bristol (TM) to Frome stopping train on the 25th July 1959. How beneficial this country branch line as a modern commuter route would have been today.

The original concept of opening this railway line was to take coal to the main marketplace of the nearby cities, and here we have a mixed freight train about to go under the passenger footbridge with an ex Great Western prairie 2-6-2T number 4131. Note the A39 Wells Road over bridge in background, c1959

The Modern Garage at White Cross with its owners Arthur Filer & Son proudly showing off a variety of petrol pumps and lubricant dispensers. The sign in the front offers free air, and parking room, ~ as distinct from space, ~ for cars and motorcycles. In the background petrol is offered at 1/4d (0.07p) per gallon. At the time that this picture was taken you could contact them by telephone on Temple Cloud 36, c1927

White Cross Lodge, June 1922

Brick House, the home of the Cam Valley Butter merchant Charles Blanning who, when this picture was taken was also a Churchwarden at Holy Trinity, High Littleton, c1934

A montage of four views of Farrington Gurney, showing in a clockwise direction, the seventeenth century Manor House; the church of St John the Baptist, rebuilt in 1843 in the Gothic style, the Wesleyan Chapel, and the main crossroads, c1910

The photographer has collected the H Matthews & Son's management and employees together to demonstrate their most modern roadside petrol station just waiting for its next customers to drive along the A39 Bristol Road. It is possible to make out the chimneys stacks of the *Farrington Inn* in the top right-hand corner of the picture, c1933

FARRINGTON GURNEY.

Collinson, Clutton.

The main A39 Bristol Road at the crossroads with Pitway Lane on the left, and Main Street (also known as High Street) on the right. Two ladies stand outside the premises run by Mrs Gait who sold groceries and drapery as well as being the village sub-post office. It is believed the other shops belong to George Clifford Clark, and the local butcher and haulier John Evans. The building on the right belongs to Henry Matthews, see petrol station on previous page. Subsequently the property became a sweet shop run by Arthur Collier, c1910

THE POST OFFICE, FARRINGTON GURNEY,

A number of years that included a World War have passed since the picture on the previous page was taken, trees have grown, and electricity has arrived, and the Gait & Co business is now run under the auspices of W E Pierce but the sedate pace of life continues, as our equine friends appear to still be the main source of motive power, c1921

FARRINGTON GURNEY

The main A39 Bristol Road with, at ninety degrees to the road, a rank of thatched cottages with two housewives encouraged out to add interest to the picture. With no traffic, we are able to see Ham Lane on the left, whilst beyond is a short rank of cottages, and then the *Farrington Inn,* c 1910. With nearly all of the properties no longer with us, and with the absence of any traffic, we are granted the opportunity of looking through a small window at a moment frozen in time.

Time has passed, the camera has been moved forward, and the thatched cottages have been demolished. Ham Lane is on the left, with beyond the *Farrington Inn* (Fredrick Penny, landlord) with its large doorway to accommodate horses and stagecoaches to pass through to the rear of the business at the time when the only means of distant travel was by such coaches that required frequent change of their motive power, especially over the Mendip hills, c1925

Triangle, Farrington Gurney.

The meeting of Bristol Road and Ham Lane forms two sides of a triangle that is then completed by the rank of cottages that face this picture, all of which, with the exception of the *Farrington Inn* have been swept away by so called progress and the insatiable appetite of the combustion engine wanting more space. Note the steam traction engine on the right, and the young girl, with older lady on the left, c1912

High St. Farrington Gurney.

For this pictorial scene of the Bristol Road, the camera has been turned completely around and we now have a wider view of the rank of cottages that were on the right on page 49 now on the left, as the road sweeps past the shops on the corner of Pitway Lane, and the junction with Main Street as it heads on towards the climb over Rush Hill, c1913

"Crossways" Tea Room ~ Frederick Gawker proprietor, ~ looking over Church Lane at its junction with Bristol Road. A motorcyclist and passenger have stopped for refreshments and to enjoy the fresh air before returning to their steed and the pleasures of the open countryside, c1935

Bristol Road when it looked so different from the hustle and bustle of today; a time when such little traffic was unable to disrupt the peace of the small community as it meandered its way through the village and past the "Crossways" Tea Room, and Mr Pierce's emporium, the Triangle and the *Farrington Inn* before heading out on its way towards the next village, c1932

Regrettably the quality of this picture is not as good as I would like, but as one of the oldest pictures in the book its historical significance warrants its inclusion, as we are seeing the same or very similar view that stagecoach drivers would have seen as they left the comfort of the *Farrington Inn* for, as far as the horses were concerned, the arduous climb up Rush Hill and the many other hills to be encountered before the coach arrived in the City of Wells, c1904

The cattle ring of Messrs. Blinman & Miles, auctioneers and valuers' market sale yard, with an event that seems to have attracted a great number of farmers and dealers out in their Sunday best, perhaps prize cattle are up for sale, c1921

The photographer has strategically positioned a lady wearing her wide brim floral hat to sit and pose in her pony and trap outside of the Parsonage, but also allowing the viewer the opportunity of looking down Main Street, sometimes also known as High Street, towards the distant rank of cottages known as Kingston Terrace, c1910. At the time of the picture Francis Kingston Blinman was in residence.

Franklyn Terrace, Farrington Gurney.

Numbers 2-6 Franklyn Terrace, ~ part of High Street or more frequently known as Main Street ~ with a local delivery cart and carter strategically positioned to help enliven this quiet country road, and the white walled *Jassamine Cottage* in the background, c1912

The sun casts shadows across the pavement, and highlights the rank of cottages known as Franklyn Terrace, as we are invited to see another group of cottages know as 1-4 Kingston Terrace, although the road is more often than not referred to as Main Road. Beyond, the first of the two taller houses is called *The Cottage* with *Merricott* next door, c1927

Three-village lads pose, as a cyclist occupies the centre of Main Street in order to skirt past the cameraman and his wooden tripod that has been set up to support his large glass plate camera. Bathed by the low sun on the left is *Southview,* which together with its neighbour, towers over the scene, c1926

Farrington colliery was originally sunk around 1782 but the coal seam was not reached for three years however, by 1786 very little work was being carried out due to the problems of flooding, and the mine was not reopened and producing coal until the 1840's. In this c1923 picture, which was probably taken after closure as the pithead winding gear is not visible, we are looking at the eastern side of the electricity generating house, and the Shaft and screens, as the internal railway, that had its own saddle tank locomotive, sweeps around to the loading bay from its connection with the main line at Old Mills siding.

In this view taken from the approach road there appears to be a fair amount of activity in this picture but is it productive, with an untidy pile of timber, the manager's car and four or five men standing idly around with their hands in their pockets. Many pits in Somerset were strike-bound during the 1921 dispute, and the owner, Sir Frank Beauchamp had already threatened to close Farrington pit if the men did not return to work. Does this picture reflect a group of pickets, whilst the manager remains in his office? c1921

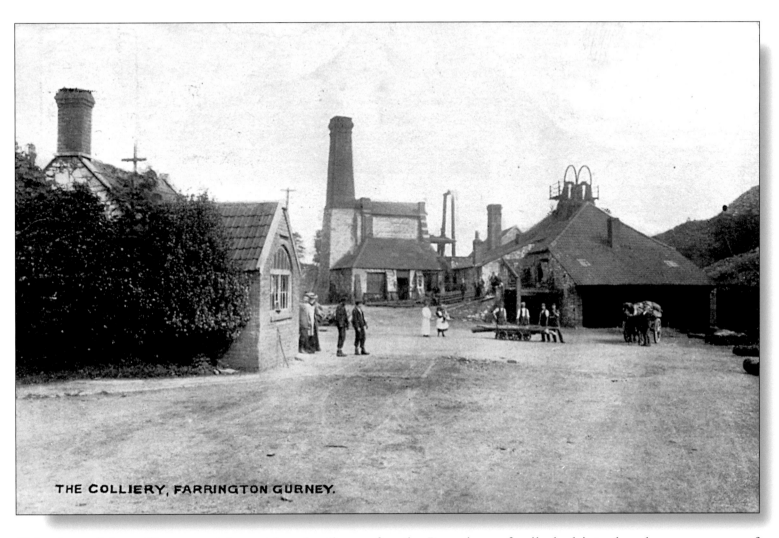

THE COLLIERY, FARRINGTON GURNEY.

This view of the colliery was taken at happier times after the Beauchamp family had introduced a programme of modernisation including the deepening of the shaft, and the opening of three profitable seams, plus the completion of the rail connection. To capture this moment in time, the photographer has grouped together carpenters and engineers, plus two or three ladies and two miners about to start their shift, c1907

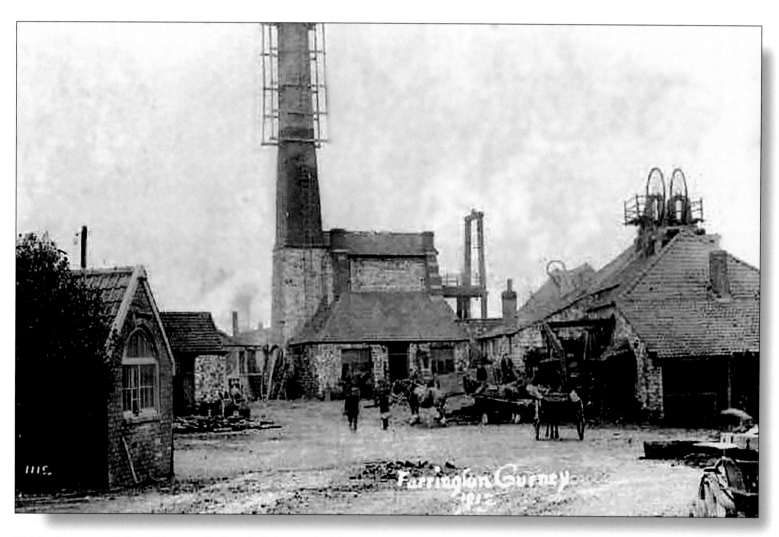

With the top of the chimney being heightened, this 1912 view of the pithead shows plenty of activity around the weighbridge with horse and carts waiting to be loaded. Although this pit had a relatively short working life, coal continued to be extracted from the ground within the parish at the nearby Old Mills and Springfield collieries that remained open until April 1966.

The lower section of Rush Hill, looking towards the crossroads, c1912

The solitary motive power of the horse drawn wagon slowly struggles up Rush Hill having passed the Marsh Lane junction and the gaunt farmhouse belonging to Rush Farm that is almost hidden by the full foliage produced at the height of the Summer of 1903.

Towards the bottom of the hill is a steam wagon no doubt trying to raise sufficient steam pressure to enable it to tackle the forthcoming gradient of a very rural Rush Hill, as we look back across the village of Farrington Gurney, c1923

Farrington Gurney

It has proven difficult to positively identify the exact location of the picture that was reproduced from a postcard used on the 11th September 1927 as a birthday card, exactly ninety years after its inclusion in this book. Believed to be taken along the A39 Bristol Road, but if you can identify the exact spot please notify the author, c1926